The symbols in the book tell you whether the animal is:

Vertebrate ■ or invertebrate ☐
Warm blooded ▲ or cold blooded △
Nocturnal ▬ or diurnal ▭
and whether the animal has babies (young born alive) ● or lays eggs ○ .

If there is no symbol ▬ or ▭ it means that the animal sometimes sleeps in the day and sometimes at night.

Scientists classify animals into groups.
The animals in this encyclopaedia fit into the following groups:

mollusc	crustacean	arachnid
insect	fish	amphibian
reptile	bird	mammal

Some of the words you may not understand are explained in the glossary on page 70 in Volume 4.

Shrimp

Common shrimp

Scientific name
**Crangon
crangon**

crustacean

☐ Invertebrate   △ Cold blooded   ◯ Lays eggs

Shrimps live in shallow water at the seaside. When they are frightened, they can quickly dig a hole and hide in the sand. They can also change colour to camouflage themselves.

Actual adult size

Home
Sand at the bottom of the sea.

Young
1600 to 14000 eggs. Female carries them stuck to her legs.

Food
Worms, small fish, dead animals.

Slow worm

Scientific name
Anguis fragilis

reptile

■ Vertebrate △ Cold blooded ○ Lays eggs ▭ Diurnal

The slow worm is not a worm or a snake. It is really
a lizard with no legs. Slow worms grow out of their
skins every six weeks. They can also shed their tails
if they need to escape.

**Adult size
to scale**

0 25 50 75 1 metre

Home
Dry places, under
stones, leaves.

Young
6 to 12 thin shelled
eggs. Hatch as soon as
laid.

Food
Worms, slugs.

Slug

Great black slug

Scientific name

Arion ater

mollusc

☐ Invertebrate △ Cold blooded ○ Lays eggs ▬ Nocturnal

A slug is really a snail without a shell. As it moves, it leaves a silver trail behind it. It has eyes on the tips of its horns. The slug pulls these horns in if you touch them.

Actual adult size

Home
Gardens, woods. Under stones and logs during the day.

Young
20 to 30 eggs.

Food
Plants. (Feeds at night.)

Snail
Garden snail

Scientific name
Helix aspersa

mollusc

☐ Invertebrate   △ Cold blooded   ○ Lays eggs   ▨ Nocturnal

A snail has a shell to protect it. The shell grows with the snail so it always fits perfectly. Every snail is both male and female at the same time. Like the slug, the snail has eyes on the tips of its horns.

Actual adult size

Home
Gardens.
Under stones during the day.

Young
20 to 30 white eggs laid in soil.

Food
Soft young garden plants. (Feeds at night.)

53

Sparrow

House sparrow

Scientific name
Passer domesticus

bird

■ Vertebrate ▲ Warm blooded ◯ Lays eggs ▭ Diurnal

There are always lots of sparrows around because sparrows have babies three times a year. Sparrows like to keep clean so they take water baths or dust baths.

Adult size to scale

0   25   50   75   1 metre

Home
Gardens, farms, near human homes. Nests in roofs of houses.

Young
3 to 5 greyish-white eggs, 3 times a year.

Food
Insects, seeds.

Spider

Garden spider

Scientific name
Araneus diadematus

arachnid

☐ Invertebrate △ Cold blooded ◯ Lays eggs

The female garden spider spins a web to trap insects. When the insects are trapped in the web, the spider wraps them in silk. Then she kills them with a poisonous bite from her fangs. She eats some of the insects. Sometimes she also eats small spiders.

Actual adult size
The male is much smaller

Home
Edges of woodland, gardens.
Lives in bushes.

Young
800 eggs laid in yellow silk cases in Autumn. Spiderlings hatch in Spring.

Food
Flies, other insects.

55

Squirrel

Grey squirrel

Scientific name

Sciurus carolinensis

mammal

■ Vertebrate ▲ Warm blooded ● Young born alive ☐ Diurnal

The squirrel is a busy animal. All day it climbs trees and looks for food. It hides this food in the ground but often forgets where it is hidden.

Adult size to scale

0   25   50   75   1 metre

Home
Woodland, parks, gardens.
Makes nest (called a drey) in treetops.

Young
3 to 4 babies born in Spring.

Food
Acorns, nuts, fruit, tree bark.

Starling

Scientific name **Sturnus vulgaris**

bird

■ Vertebrate　▲ Warm blooded　◯ Lays eggs　▢ Diurnal

A starling can look a dull bird but in the sunlight its feathers shine. The starling can copy the sounds of other birds. It is also a bit of a bully and it fights other birds for food.

Adult size to scale

0　25　50　75　1 metre

Home
Fields, gardens.
Nests in hollow trees.

Young
5 to 7 light blue eggs.

Food
Almost anything.

57

Stickleback

Three spined stickleback

Scientific name
Gasterosteus aculeatus

fish

■ Vertebrate △ Cold blooded ○ Lays eggs

Sticklebacks are also called tiddlers. They are little fish which have an unusual habit. They build nests. The nests look like tunnels, made from water weeds. Sticklebacks build these nests at the bottom of ponds.

Actual adult size

Home
Rivers, streams, ponds.
Nest made of water weeds.

Young
50 to 150 eggs.
Male protects eggs until they hatch.

Food
Small water creatures.

Swan

Mute swan

Scientific name
Cygnus olor

bird

■ Vertebrate   ▲ Warm blooded   ○ Lays eggs   ▭ Diurnal

Swans are the biggest and heaviest birds in Britain. Swans are unusual because they stay with the same mate for the whole of their lives. A male swan is called a cob and a female is called a pen.

Adult size to scale

0   25   50   75   1 metre

Home
Rivers, lakes.
Big nest of twigs on bank.

Young
4 to 7 white eggs.
Baby swans are called cygnets.

Food
Water weed, seeds, insects.

59

Swift

Scientific name
Apus apus

bird

■ Vertebrate   ▲ Warm blooded   ○ Lays eggs   ▭ Diurnal

The swift is a fast flying bird. It twists and turns high in the air. Each swift flies over a million miles during its life. They migrate to Africa in the Winter.

Adult size to scale

0   25   50   75   1 metre

Home
Around buildings
or cliffs.
Nests in roof spaces.

Young
2 to 3 smooth white
eggs.

Food
Small insects caught
and eaten in the air.

Thrush
Song thrush

Scientific name
Turdus philomelos

bird

■ Vertebrate   ▲ Warm blooded   ○ Lays eggs   ▭ Diurnal

The thrush is a songbird which eats snails. It breaks open the shells by bashing them against a stone. A thrush often has a favourite stone which it always uses. This is called its anvil.

Adult size to scale

0   25   50   75   1 metre

Home
Woodland, parks, gardens.
Nests in bushes.

Young
4 to 6 light blue speckled eggs.

Food
Worms, snails, insects.

61

Toad

Common toad

Scientific name

Bufo bufo

amphibian

■ Vertebrate   △ Cold blooded   ○ Lays eggs

Toads do not leap or jump like frogs, they walk. In Spring female toads walk back to the ponds where they were born. This is where they want to lay their eggs. Many toads are killed as they cross the roads on the way home.

Adult size to scale

0   25   50   75   1 metre

Home
Ponds, rivers, damp places.
Hibernates under logs or stones.

Young
Up to 7000 eggs (toadspawn) laid in water.

Food
Insects, worms.

Vole

Bank vole

Scientific name

Clethrionomys glareolus

mammal

■ Vertebrate ▲ Warm blooded ● Young born alive ☐ Diurnal

The vole is a small animal. It has a very short life. Most voles die before they are a year old. They are killed and eaten by kestrels, owls and other predators.

Adult size to scale

0   25   50   75   1 metre

Home
Fields, hedges, woodland.
Underground nest.

Young
3 to 6 babies in a litter. Young can have their own babies when 4 to 5 weeks old.

Food
Grass, plants, seeds.

Wagtail

Pied wagtail

Scientific name

Motacilla alba yarrellii

bird

■ Vertebrate ▲ Warm blooded ○ Lays eggs ▭ Diurnal

The wagtail has a tail which wags up and down. Wagtails have a special way of moving. They do not hop like other birds. They run. When they fly they take off quickly but they often dip down suddenly.

Adult size to scale

0   25   50   75   1 metre

Home
Near water, near human homes. Nests in gaps in rocks under bridges.

Young
4 to 6 speckled eggs.

Food
Small flies and other insects.

Wasp
Common wasp

Scientific name
Vespula vulgaris

insect

☐ Invertebrate △ Cold blooded ◯ Lays eggs ▱ Diurnal

The black and yellow colours of the wasp help to protect it. They warn other animals to keep away. The female wasp can sting to protect herself. Males cannot sting.

Actual adult size
The queen is bigger

Home
Wasps live in colonies. Nests in hollow trees or in roofs.

Young
Queen lays hundreds of eggs.

Food
Sweet things, nectar from flowers, insects.

Water spider

Scientific name
Argyroneta aquatica

arachnid

☐ Invertebrate   △ Cold blooded   ○ Lays eggs

This is the only British spider that lives under water. The female spins a web under water. She fills the web with air. This web full of air is called an air bell. The spider lives in the air bell.

Actual adult size

Home
Ponds and water-filled ditches.

Young
2 to 100 eggs laid in air bell.

Food
Small water creatures.

Weasel

Scientific name
Mustela nivalis

mammal

■ Vertebrate   ▲ Warm blooded   ● Young born alive

The weasel is small but it is a fierce hunter. It kills its prey with a bite at the back of its head. The female guards her babies well. If there is danger, she moves them one by one to a safe place.

Adult size to scale

0   25   50   75   1 metre

Home
Fields, woodland.
Underground nest.

Young
5 to 6 babies in a litter.

Food
Mice, voles, rabbits, baby birds.

Woodlouse

Scientific name
Porcellio scaber

crustacean

☐ Invertebrate △ Cold blooded ○ Lays eggs ▨ Nocturnal

The woodlouse has to live in damp and dark places.

It would die if it stayed too long in the sunshine.

Some woodlice roll up into a ball if they are attacked.

Actual adult size

Home
Woodland, parks, gardens. Under logs and stones. In rotten wood.

Young
Lays 7 to 200 eggs. Baby woodlice carried underneath mother.

Food
Plants - dead or alive.

Woodpecker
Great spotted woodpecker

Scientific name
Dendrocopus major

bird

■ Vertebrate ▲ Warm blooded ○ Lays eggs ▭ Diurnal

Woodpeckers peck at trees. They peck at the bark to find the insects in the wood. They peck very loudly in Spring to warn other woodpeckers to keep away.

Adult size to scale

0   25   50   75   1 metre

Home
Woodland, parks.
Nests in holes it makes in trees.

Young
5 to 7 white eggs.

Food
Insects from under bark of trees.

69

Glossary of words found in The Introductory Encyclopaedia of British Wild Animals

Amphibian   An amphibian is an animal which can live in the water or on land.

Antlers   Antlers are the horns of a deer. They look like the branches of a tree.

Arachnid   An arachnid is an animal which has four pairs of legs.

Bird   A bird is an animal that has wings and feathers. All birds lay eggs and nearly all birds can fly.

Camouflaged   An animal is camouflaged when it looks like its surroundings. A camouflaged animal is very difficult to see.

Cold blooded   Cold blooded animals have the same temperature as their surroundings. They hibernate or die if the weather gets very cold.

Colony   A colony is a large organised group of the same sort of creature.

Crustacean   Crustaceans are animals which have a hard shell and jointed legs.

Diurnal   Diurnal animals stay awake during the day and go to sleep at night.

Dung   Dung is the waste products of an animal's body. Some people call it dirt or manure.

Female   A female animal is a girl animal.

Fish   Fish live in water all of the time. They have a skin made of scales and they usually have fins.

Grub   The babies of some insects are called grubs.

Hibernates   An animal hibernates when it sleeps all through the winter.

Insect   Insects are small and sometimes have wings. They always have six legs.

Invertebrate   An invertebrate is an animal without a backbone.

Litter   A litter is a group of babies born at the same time to the same mother.

Male   A male animal is a boy animal.

Mammal	A mammal is a warm blooded animal with a backbone. Female mammals are able to feed their babies with milk.
Mating	Mating is a male and female animal joining together to make a baby.
Migrate	An animal migrates when it goes away to a warmer country.
Mollusc	Molluscs have soft bodies with no backbone. Some (like snails) have a shell but some (like slugs) have no shell.
Nectar	Nectar is a sweet food that is made by flowers.
Nocturnal	Nocturnal animals sleep during the day but are awake at night.
Pincers	Pincers are like long claws or hands.
Predator	A predator is any animal which catches other animals and eats them.
Queen	The queen is the largest insect in a colony. There is only one queen in each colony and she lays all the eggs.
Reptile	A reptile is a cold blooded animal with a dry scaly skin. Reptiles usually live in warm places. They lay eggs.
Scientific name	A scientific name is the name scientists have given to an animal. The same scientific name can be understood all over the world.
Shed	Some animals can shed or break away from bits of their bodies and leave them behind. This helps them to escape from an enemy who is holding on to them.
Vertebrate	A vertebrate is any animal that has a backbone.
Vomiting	Vomiting means being sick.
Warm blooded	Warm blooded animals can keep their body heat at the same temperature in any weather.
Wingspan	Wingspan is the distance from the tip of one wing to the tip of the other wing when the wings are spread out.
Worker	Workers are the ants, bees and wasps who keep the nest tidy and fetch food back to a colony.

Index of Volumes 1-4